Quick Draw
Minibeasts

KINGFISHER

How to use this book

1. Trace the grid opposite. You can use any size of paper as long as the grid proportions are the same as the one in this book. The grid squares will help you position your drawing and ensure the different stages are correctly scaled.

2. Use a light pencil line to draw. That way you can rub out the lines much more easily.

3. Copy the shapes in step one, then add the new shapes in step two and so on. As you add each step, your picture will begin to take shape.

4. When you have copied each step, rub out the extra lines from the earlier step – to eventually reveal the final shape (as shown in the final step).

5. Now colour in your finished picture.

As you become more confident, you may find that you don't need the grid squares any more. You may wish to add your own finishing touches to the illustrations, such as background plants, to create a scene.

Caterpillar

Step 1

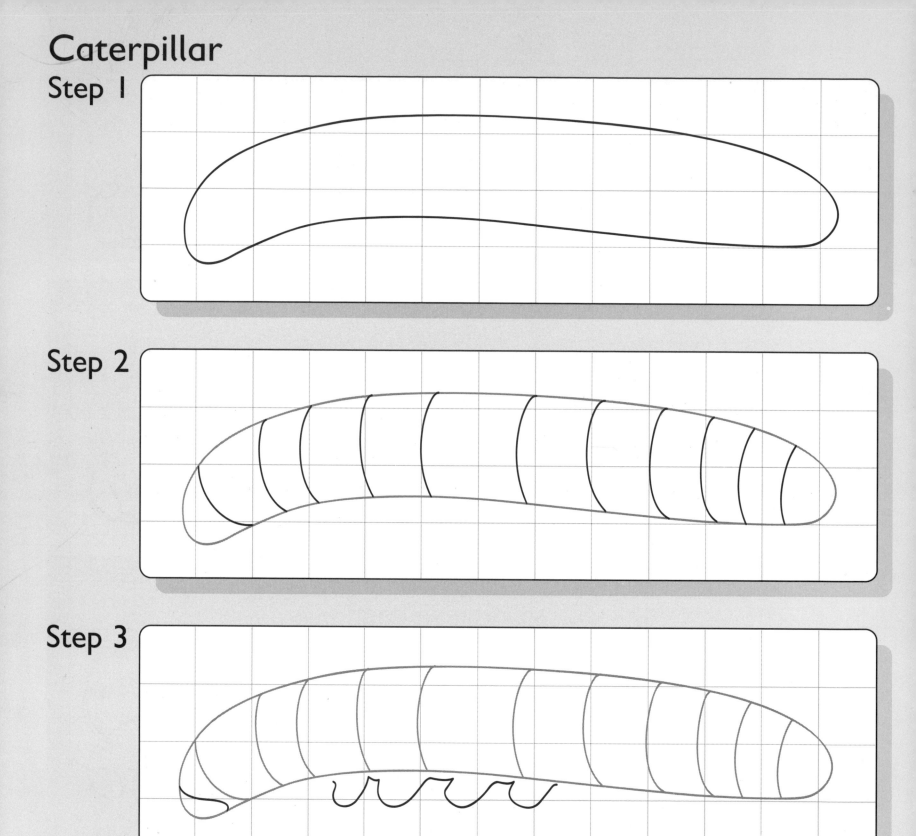

Step 2

Step 3

Step 4

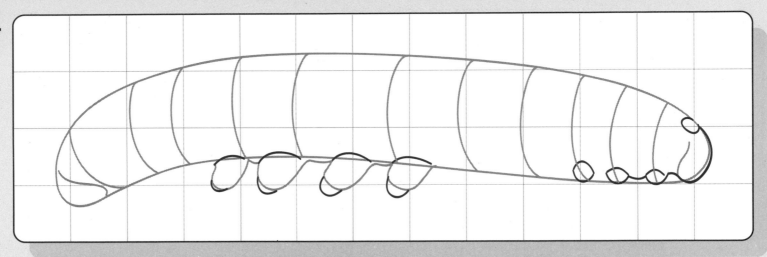

Step 5

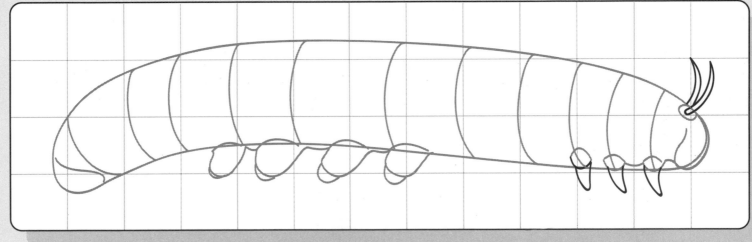

Step 6

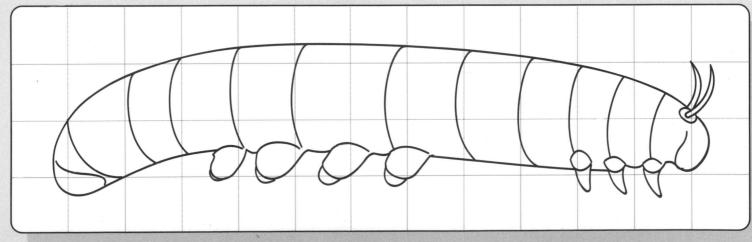

Dragonfly

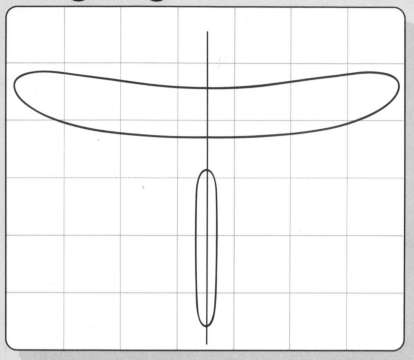

Step 1

Step 2

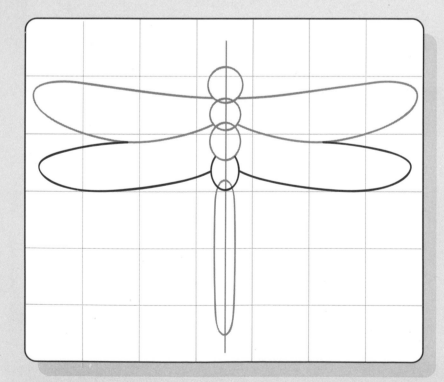

Step 3

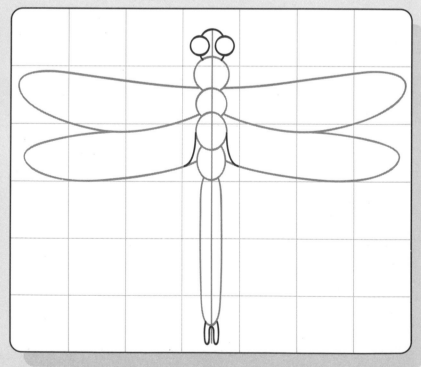

Step 4

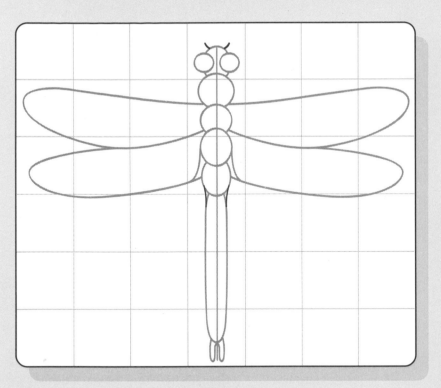

Step 5

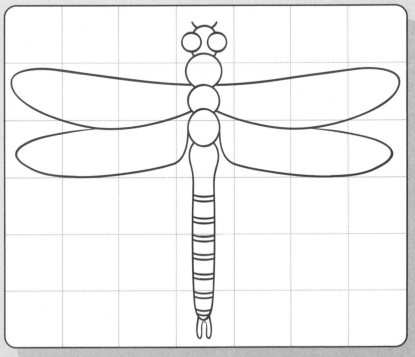

Step 6

Step 7

Step 8

Scorpion

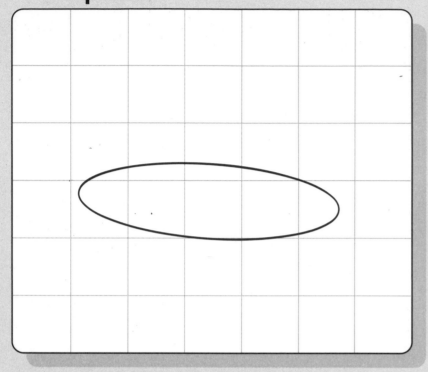

Step 1

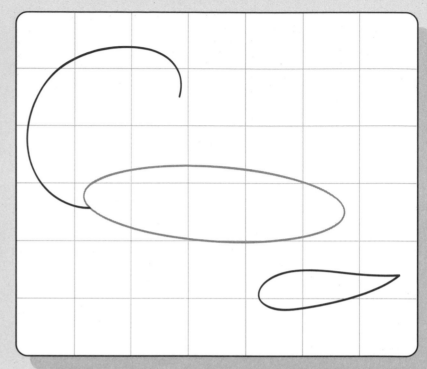

Step 2

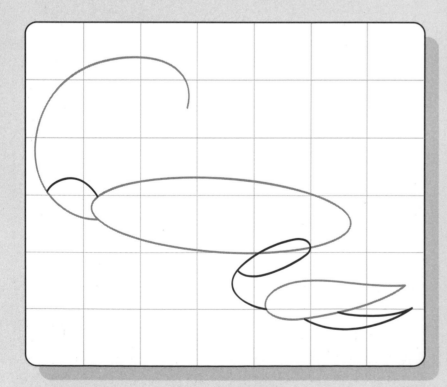

Step 3

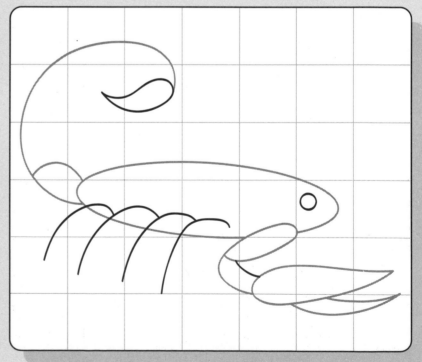

Step 4

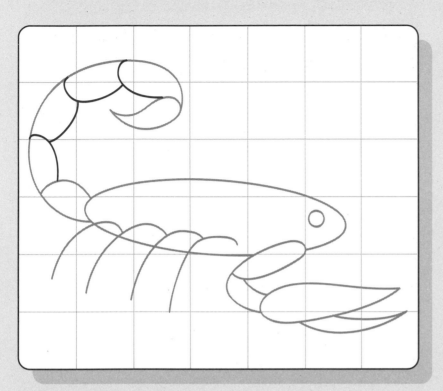

Step 5

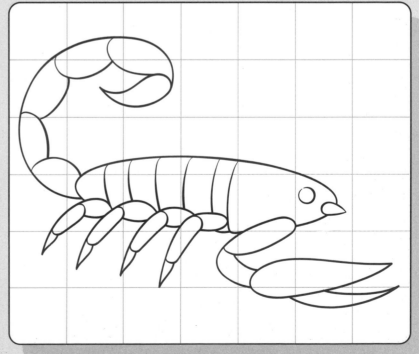

Step 6

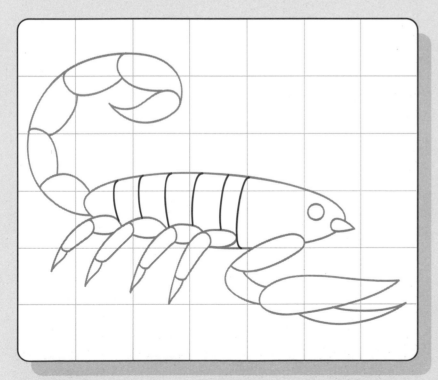

Step 7

Step 8

Snail

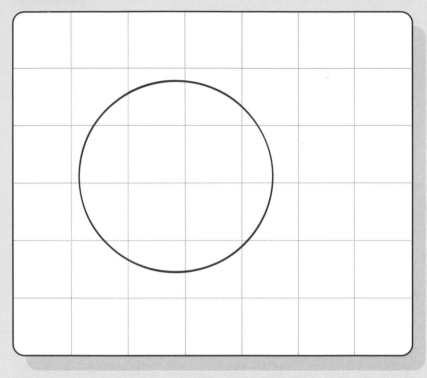

Step 1

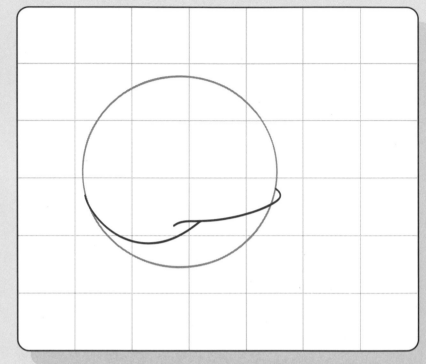

Step 2

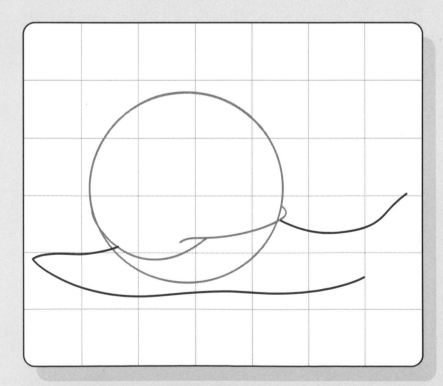

Step 3

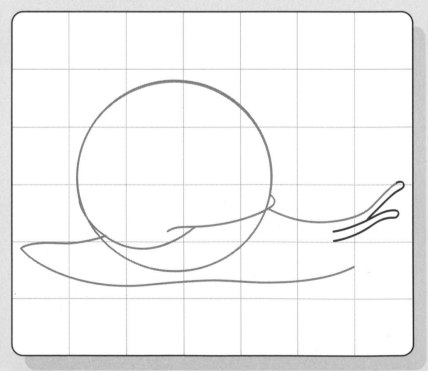

Step 4

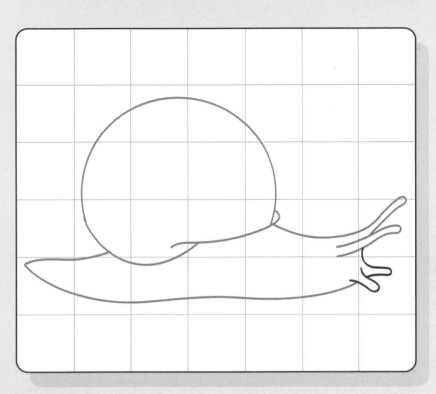

Step 5

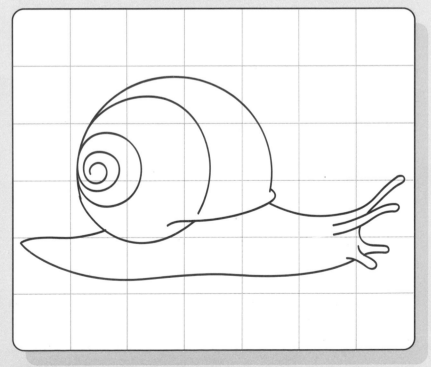

Step 6

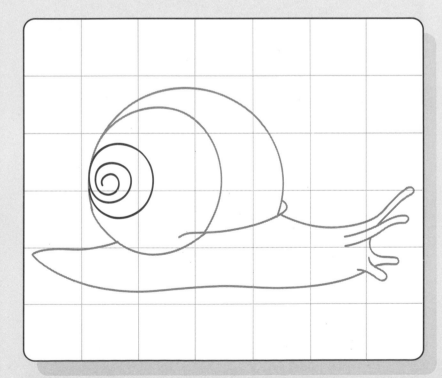

Step 7

Step 8

Earthworm

Step 1

Step 2

Step 3

Step 4

Step 5

Step 6

Ant

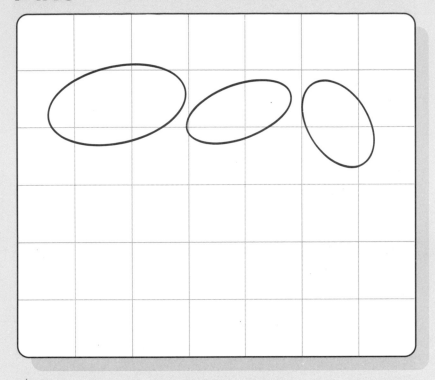

Step 1

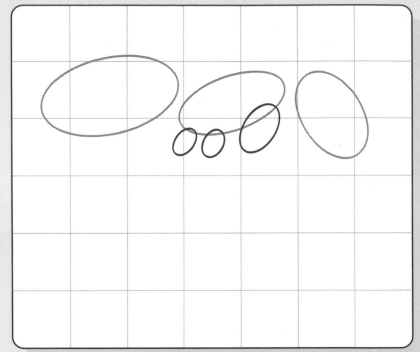

Step 2

Step 3

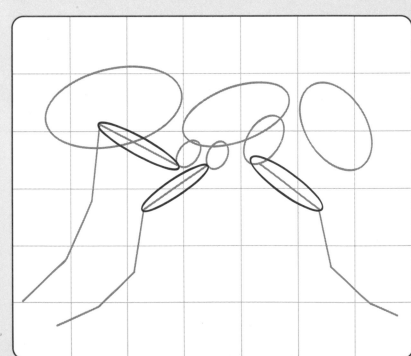

Step 4

Step 5

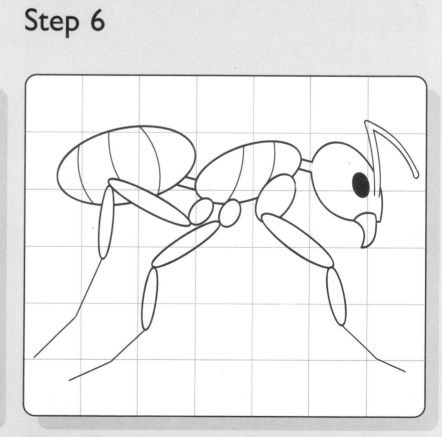

Step 6

Step 7

Step 8

Earwig

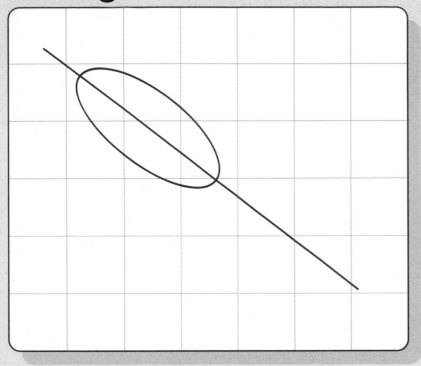

Step 1

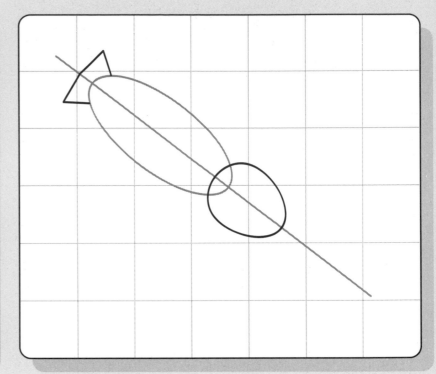

Step 2

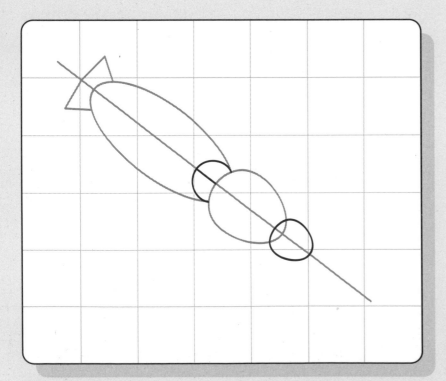

Step 3

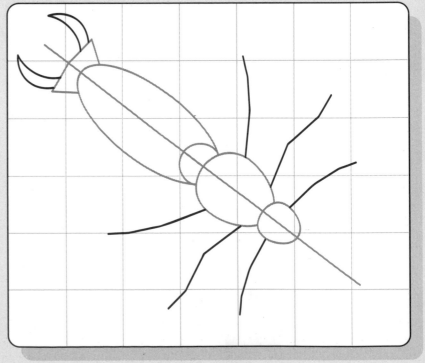

Step 4

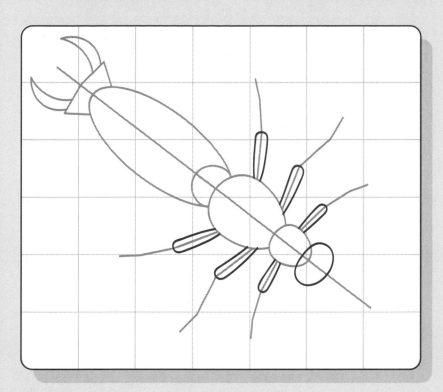

Step 5

Step 6

Step 7

Step 8

Spider

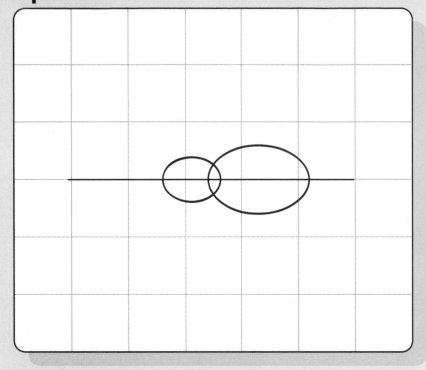

Step 1

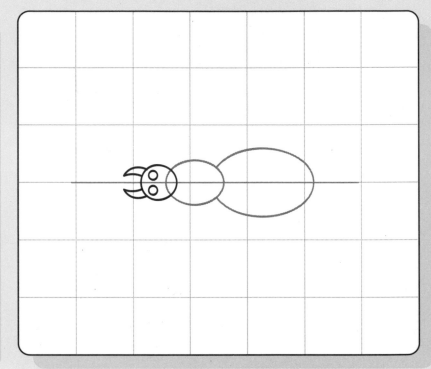

Step 2

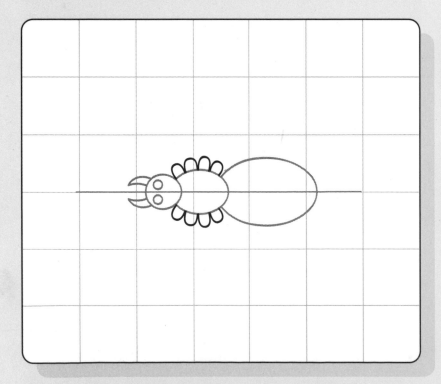

Step 3

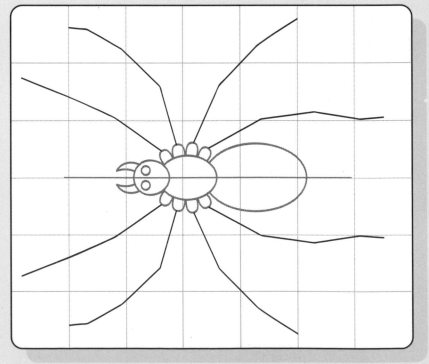

Step 4

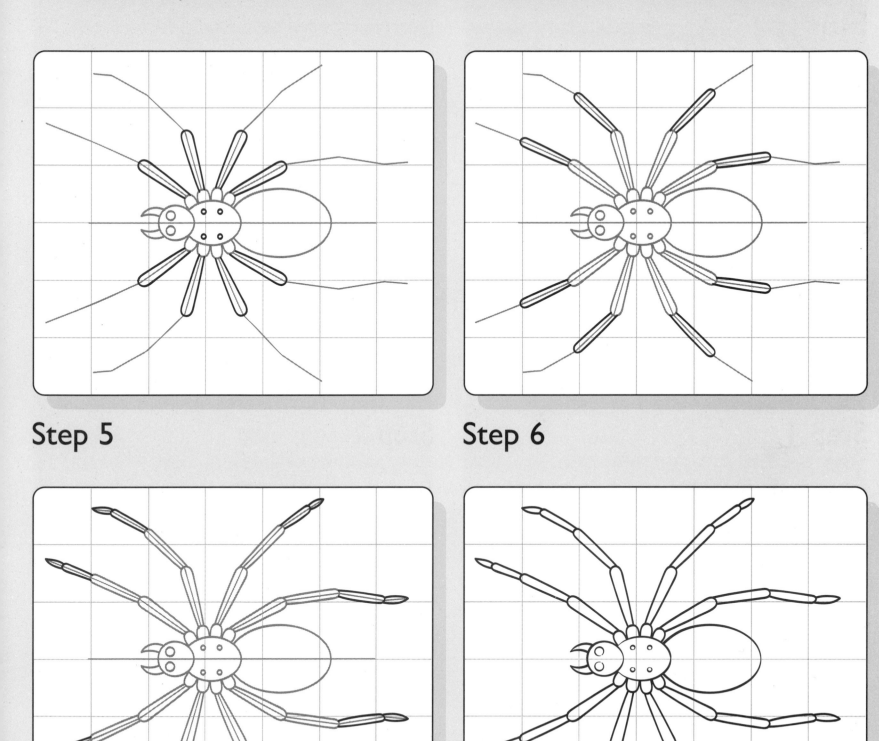

Step 5

Step 6

Step 7

Step 8

Fly

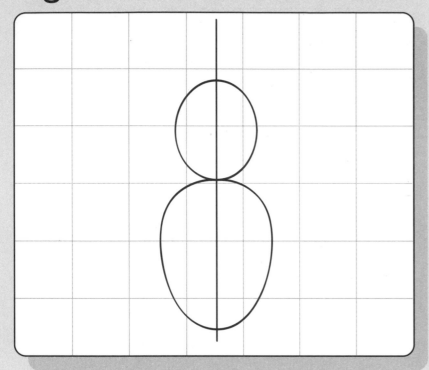

Step 1

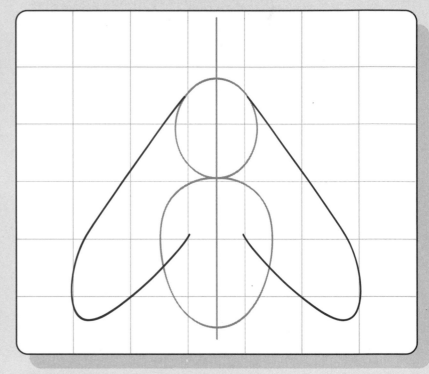

Step 2

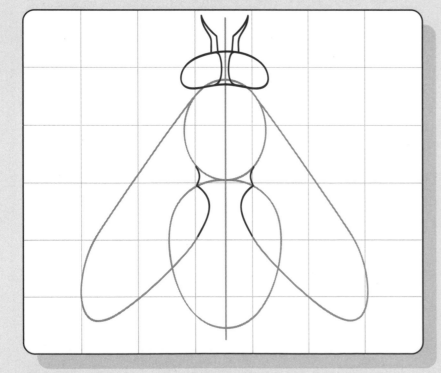

Step 3

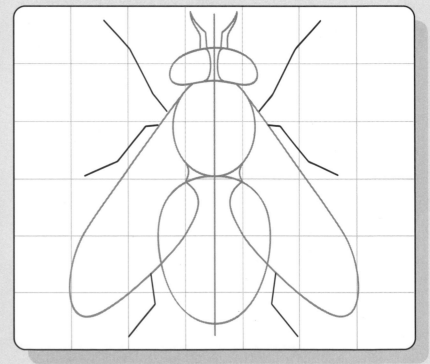

Step 4

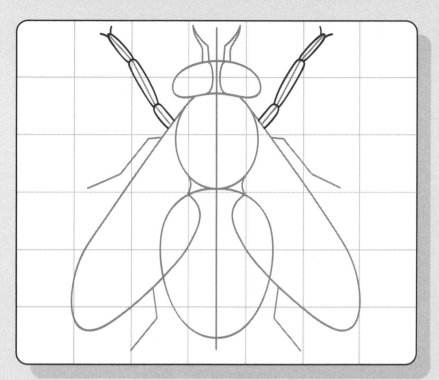

Step 5

Step 6

Step 7

Step 8

Ladybird

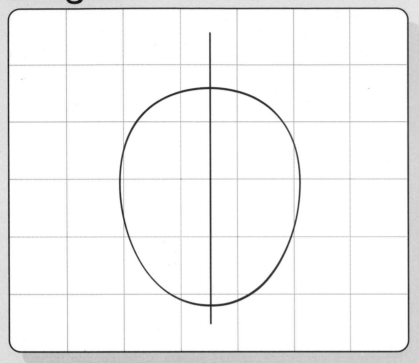

Step 1

Step 2

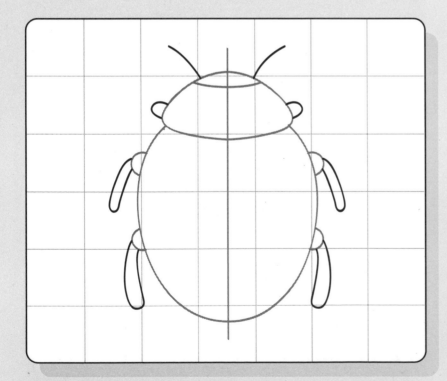

Step 3

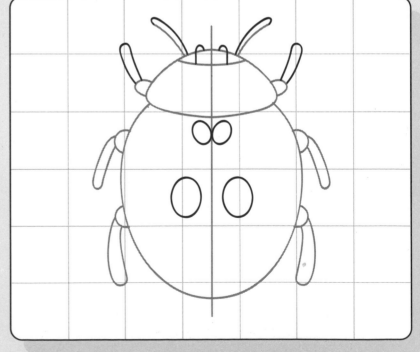

Step 4

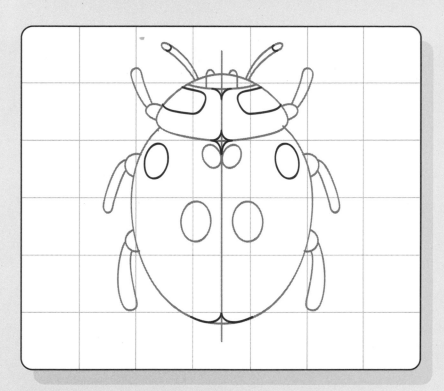

Step 5

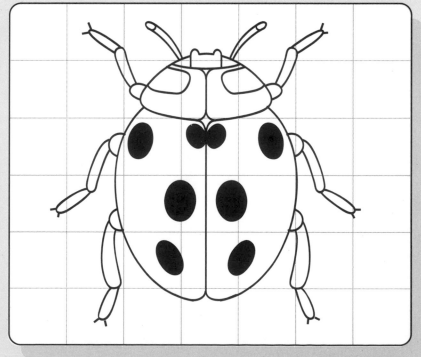

Step 6

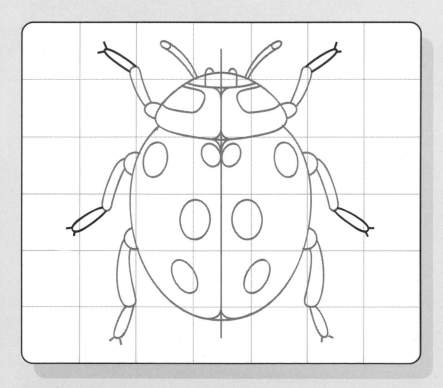

Step 7

Step 8

Beetle

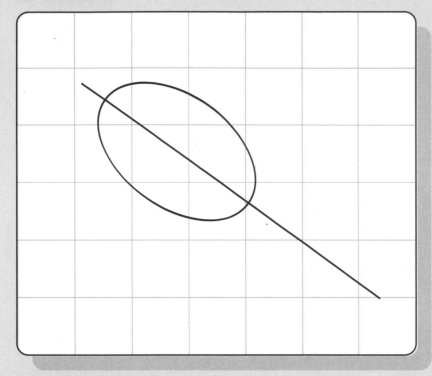

Step 1

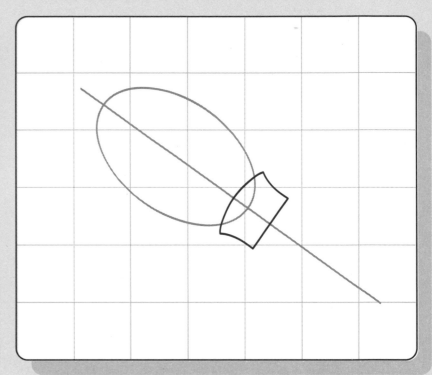

Step 2

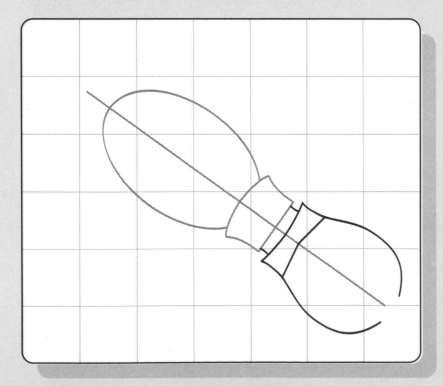

Step 3

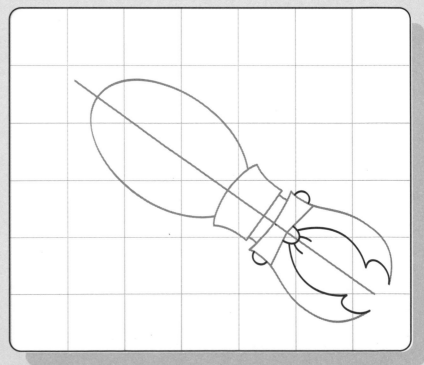

Step 4

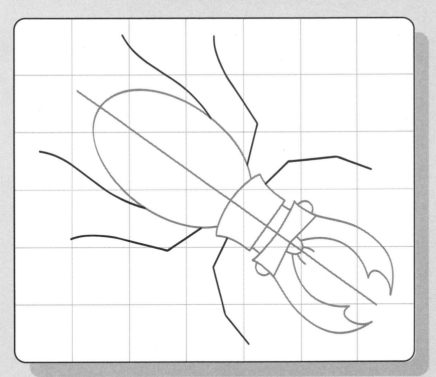

Step 5

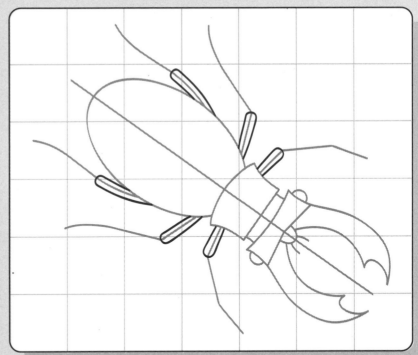

Step 6

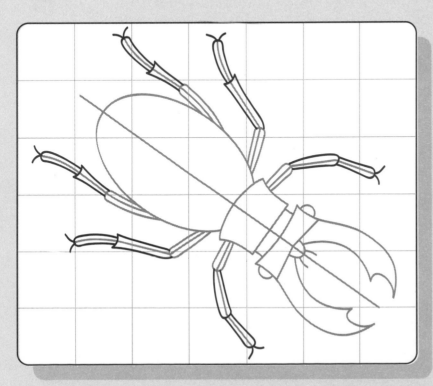

Step 7

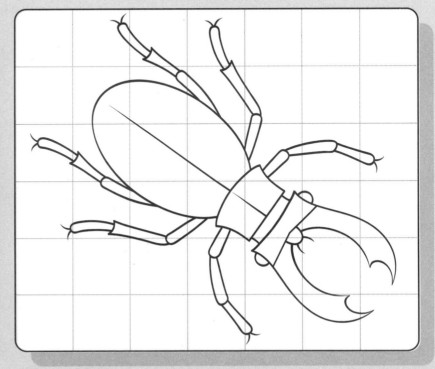

Step 8

Bee

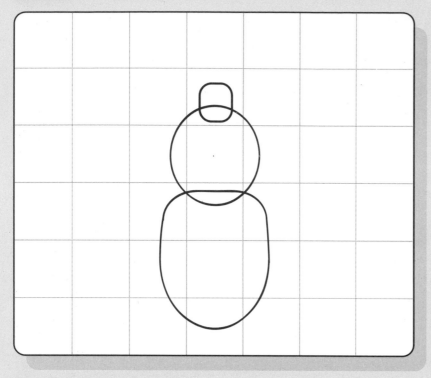

Step 1

Step 2

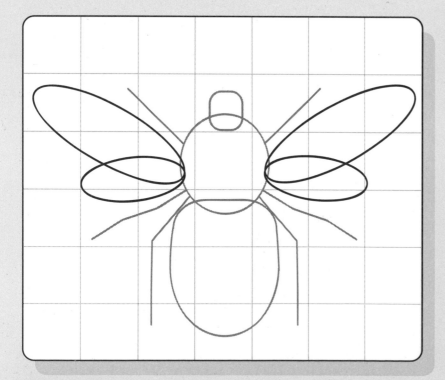

Step 3

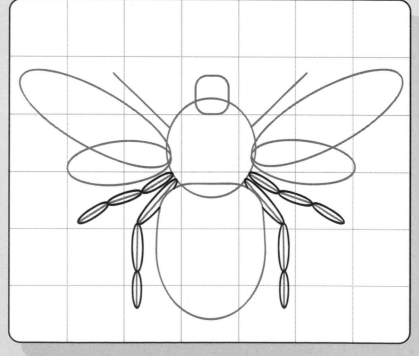

Step 4

Step 5

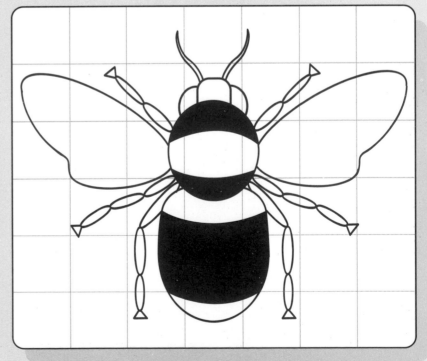

Step 6

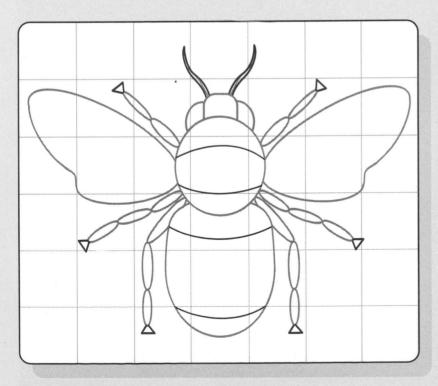

Step 7

Step 8

Butterfly

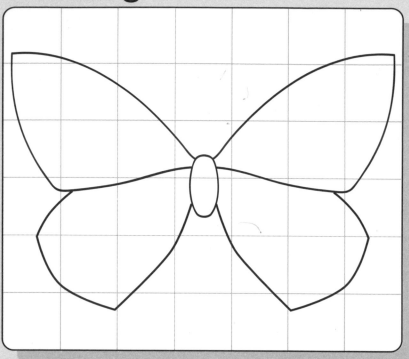

Step 1

Step 2

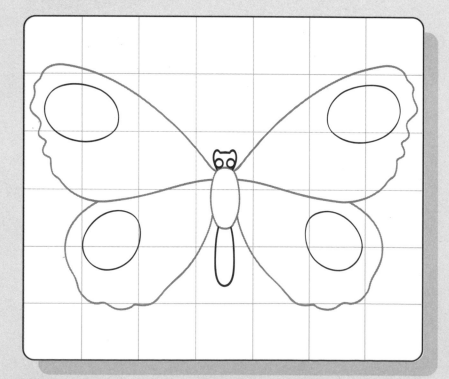

Step 3

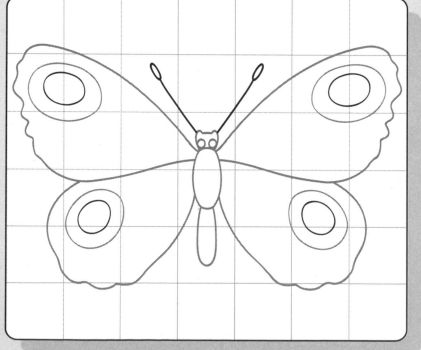

Step 4

Step 5

Step 6

Step 7

Step 8

Grasshopper

Step 1

Step 2

Step 3

Step 4

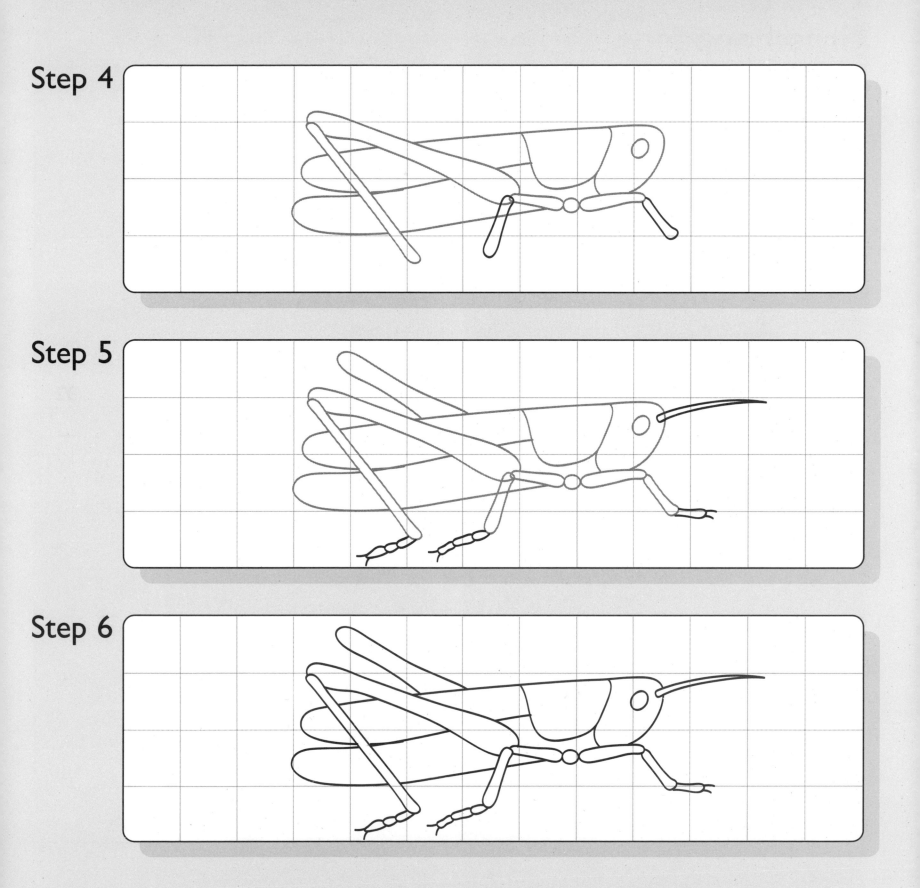

Step 5

Step 6

KINGFISHER

First published 2008 by Kingfisher
an imprent of Macmillan Children's Books
a division of Macmillan Publishers Limited
20 New Wharf Road, London N1 9RR
Basingstoke and Oxford
Associated companies throughout the world
www.panmacmillan.com

ISBN: 978-0-7534-1609-9

Copyright © Macmillan Publishers Limited 2008

Produced by The Peter Bull Studio

1 3 5 7 9 8 6 4 2
1TR/1107/THOM/IGS(SCHOY)/120BLT/C

A CIP catalogue record for this book is available from the British Library.

Visit **www.panmacmillan.com** to read more about all our books
and to buy them. You will also find features, author interviews and
news of any author events, and you can sign up for e-newsletters
so that you're always first to hear about our new releases.

Printed in India